THE CHRISTIAN DRAMA QUEEN MENTALITY

Claudette Dixon and Kimberly Moses

Copyright © 2021 by **Claudette Dixon and Kimberly Moses**

All rights reserved. No part of this publication may be reproduced, distributed or transmitted in any form or by any means, including photocopying, recording, or other electronic or mechanical methods, without the prior written permission of the publisher, except in the case of brief quotations embodied in critical reviews and certain other noncommercial uses permitted by copyright law. For permission requests, write to the publisher, addressed "Attention: Permissions Coordinator," at the address below.

Claudette Dixon and Kimberly Moses/Rejoice Essential Publishing

PO BOX 512

Effingham, SC 29541

www.republishing.org

Unless otherwise indicated, scripture is taken from the King James Version.'

The Holy Bible, English Standard Version (ESV) is adapted from the Revised Standard Version of the Bible, copyright Division of Christian Education of the National Council of the Churches of Christ in the U.S.A. All rights reserved.

The Christian Drama Queen Mentality/Claudette Dixon and Kimberly Moses

ISBN-13: 978-1-952312-80-9

LCCN: 2021942501

DEDICATION

This book wouldn't be possible without the inspiration of the Holy Spirit. 2 Timothy 3:16-17 says, "All scripture is given by inspiration of God, and is profitable for doctrine, for reproof, for correction, for instruction in righteousness: That the man of God may be perfect, thoroughly furnished unto all good works."

TABLE OF CONTENTS

INTRODUCTION...1

CHAPTER 1: What is a Christian Drama Queen Mentality?.................4

CHAPTER 2: How to Identify Drama Queens and their Mentality.............11

CHAPTER 3: The Personality Disorder: Symptoms of a Drama Queen.........19

CHAPTER 4: Do Men Possess the Drama Queen Mindset? Are Drama Queens One Gender?......................25

CHAPTER 5: How to Deal with a Drama Queen?............................32

CHAPTER 6: The Commonalities of Drama Queens and Narcissists..................37

CHAPTER 7: How Will Drama Queens Control You?..................43

CHAPTER 8: How to Get Free from a

Drama Queen Mentality?...............49

ABOUT THE AUTHORS..55
    Claudette Dixon.............................55
    Kimberly Moses..............................59

INTRODUCTION

CLAUDETTE'S PERSPECTIVE

This book was birthed out of the concern for all people, especially women who may have the Christian drama queen mentality or know someone with the qualities of a drama Queen. This book is geared for Christians, and non-Christians. I was invited to speak on Prophetess Kimberly Moses' platform online and ministered on the subject, "It's time to embrace your prophetic destiny." The Holy Spirit began to download the revelation, knowledge, or insight of what hinders a lot of people in moving forward to their destiny. This book gives clarity and knowledge that unravels the attributes of drama queen mentality and teaches how to identify them.

KIMBERLY'S PERSPECTIVE

One night, Apostle Claudette Dixon was a guest on my broadcast "Hot Topics." Usually, God allows me to interview the speaker, but that night, He said to flow. As I began to prepare for the broadcast, He gave me a list of words to write down so I could release them.

A few minutes before we went LIVE, the apostle and I were in the back studio of Streamyard. I told her what the Lord said, and she agreed. When we started, the atmosphere was charged. Immediately, I began to feel contractions as if I was actually giving birth. Several women testified that they felt those contractions and that the weighty presence of God's glory or "Kavod" sat upon them. Then Apostle Dixon began to release this powerful revelation about Christian Drama Queens. I was blown away and we began to take turns prophesying to the people on the broadcasts. Before we ended the video, we decided to write this book together. Days after the broadcast ended, testimonies were coming forth and I knew that we had Heaven's seal of approval on this book.

As you read the pages of this book, we will discuss the following:

- What is a Christian Drama Queen Mentality?
- How to Identify Drama Queens and their Mentality
- The Personality Disorder: Symptoms of a Drama Queen
- Do Men Possess the Drama Queen Mindset? Are Drama Queens One Gender?
- How to Deal with a Drama Queen?
- The Commonalities of Drama Queens and Narcissists
- How Will Drama Queens Control You?
- How to Get Free from a Drama Queen Mentality?

CHAPTER 1

WHAT IS A CHRISTIAN DRAMA QUEEN MENTALITY?

Christian Drama Queen Mentality: Hindrances to Women of Prophetic Destiny

CLAUDETTE'S PERSPECTIVE

Are you a drama queen? Or a Christian drama queen. What is a drama queen? This is a person, specifically a woman needing validation and the pump up to keep going. Everything revolves around her and benefits her, even her prayer life. In other words, it's ALL about you! Regardless of how someone else feels and what they are going through, a drama queen cares nothing about anyone. A Christian drama queen has a mentality that has been conditioned to believe they will do anything to get and keep attention no matter what type of arena. This type of mentality keeps a woman stagnant in that it confines them to a limited view and forward movement of ALL they can have and be. Their identity is marred and shaped by illegal thoughts. They have put on a mask to disguise themselves as if they are very humble. Many Christian drama queens have learned to play the role of a devout Christian or woman of God. They have learned the Word of God very well. They know what to say to draw and keep your attention to gain your trust and validation. If there was an Academy Award for churches, this person with the drama queen mentality will surely get an Oscar. In other words, a Christian drama queen is simply a hypocrite. The word hypocrite in Greek means stage-actor. It is a phrase that connotes both acting and overacting. The drama queen mentality is very religious in that it gives disapproval to people who break religious regulations. It is a personality disorder.

The drama queen needs personal attention and approval, either from God or from their social group. You can be a religious or non-religious drama queen any time you build yourself up by wanting others to see you as a diva. In this day and age, drama queens take all kinds of Scriptures out of context or make up new rules. Thriving on drama leads to instability, anxiety, and dissatisfaction. Let's look a little closer at the specific gender of a drama queen, so we do not fixate ourselves on the woman only as a drama queen.

Why do some people need drama? The need for drama stemmed partly from a need for attention. Some people feel unnoticed in life or felt bypassed by other people. There is a very thin line between a narcissist and a Christian drama queen. Creating drama was one way of gaining attention. People with a need for drama often show personality disorders which include borderline Narcissistic Personality Disorder. Let's take a look further into some of the behavior of a drama queen or narcissistic personality.

1.Learned Behavior:

This behavior is being taught where drama is the central role in the home. You learn this is how people act. Without having a role model or a stable relationship can cloud your view of how people might internalize that people show love and affection through unstable and dramatic behavior.

2. Self-Sabotaging Behaviors:

Whether the trauma you've experienced is physical, emotional, or sexual abuse, the Christian drama queens uses these experiences to recreate dramatic situations. Ultimately, this is self-destructive behavior. It is very awkward to feel happy and content while you are living in dramatic situations. Low self-esteem can be found within this type because of the results of past trauma.

3. Manipulation and Control:

Creating drama is one way to control others. Instead of being open and honest with other people, you draw them into drama. You then create reasons to fight with them. Finally, you make a person feel bad or guilty about the way they acted towards you.

KIMBERLY'S PERSPECTIVE

A Christian Drama queen has the following characteristics: Self-centeredness, messiness, and manipulation. Christians must be Christ-centered. We must follow Christ and be imitators of Him (1 Corinthians 11:1).

1 Peter 2:21 (ESV) says, "For to this you have been called, because Christ also suffered for you, leaving you an example, so that you might follow in his steps."

However, Christian drama queens are only concerned about themselves. They feel like the world revolves around them. They may have the title of a Christian but lack the fruit that is mentioned in Galatians 5:22-23.

22 But the fruit of the Spirit is love, joy, peace, longsuffering, gentleness, goodness, faith,

23 Meekness, temperance: against such there is no law.

Instead of having fruits of the Holy Spirit, they manifest fruits of the flesh that are listed in Galatians 5: 19-21.

19 Now the works of the flesh are manifest, which are these, adultery, fornication, uncleanness, lasciviousness,

20 Idolatry, witchcraft, hatred, variance, emulations, wrath, strife, seditions, heresies,

21 Envyings, murders, drunkenness, revellings, and such like: of the which I tell you before, as I have also told you in time past, that they which do such things shall not inherit the kingdom of God.

Since Christian drama queens don't demonstrate God's love, they are rude. I have met many women who didn't show themselves to be friendly. I can recall going to a particular church. When I went to hug them, they pulled away and rolled their eyes at me.

Next, these women don't have the joy of the Lord and being around them, you can feel their negative energy. You will actually start to feel heavy and miserable just like them. The joy of the Lord is our strength (Nehemiah 8:10), so there are no excuses why we should be walking around depressed.

These women aren't peacemakers, but they are instigators and will escalate any problem. We are called to be peacemakers and must choose and pick our battles. A fool gives full vent to their anger (Proverbs 29:11) and people are watching us to see how we are going to respond. I have witnessed many people ask questions or gossip to provoke anger in others because they love drama.

Christian drama queens aren't patient and often move ahead of God. They will place unrealistic demands on others just to have their way. We must seek God in everything so we can stay in His will because it's the safest place to be.

Next, people with the Christian drama queen spirit aren't gentle and they mistreat God's people. They will curse you out and tear you down with their words. A cursing Christian is an oxymoron. Salt and freshwater do not come out of the same well (James 3:11). I remember this so-called Christian cursed me out when I first got saved. I ran for the hills, blocked them, and never looked back.

Christian Drama queens are caught up in getting the glory and recognition. They must realize that it is about Christ and not them. We are to be hidden in Christ (Colossians 3:3). If they do good works, there is a motive behind it. We must be selfless. We have to put others' needs before our own.

Pride is another fruit that Christian drama queens manifest. Their heads are swollen due to people complimenting or worshipping them. They rarely point people back to Jesus and they often feel like they can do things in their own strength. If they can't have their way with an individual, they will find someone they can easily control. Once they are done with an individual, they will kick them to the curb.

CHAPTER 2

HOW TO IDENTIFY DRAMA QUEENS AND THEIR MENTALITY

CLAUDETTE'S PERSPECTIVE

Let's identify some things about a Christian drama queen:

She/He makes a big deal out of little things.
She/He stirs things up by gossiping and deception to cause arguments and trouble with others.
She/He never sees herself as part of the problem.
She/He is never satisfied unless she gets her way.
She/He likes being the center of attention and gets a thrill from the chaos she creates.

The Bible has Christian drama queens. So, let's take a look closely at some women that had a Christian drama queen mentality.

Rachel, Jacob's wife, was an enemy against her sister Leah. Jacob loved Rachel the most, but she wasn't able to have children. Leah had numerous children, but Rachel pleaded and stated, "Give me children or I will die (Genesis 30:1)."

Jezebel was a very jealous, envious, vengeful drama queen. She was married to King Ahab. Jezebel was very manipulative. Her husband Ahab envied and desired their neighbor's vineyard. The owner of the vineyard declined to give the vineyard to King Ahab. Jezebel falsely accused him of cursing God and the King. It ended in the neighbor's death (1 Kings 21:5-16). Jezebel worked her drama queen magic to try and manipulate her neighbor even after the neighbor told King Ahab that he wouldn't give up his vineyard. As a result, it ended very horribly.

Queen Vashti was also a drama queen in that she thought she was more than anyone else. She disrespected her husband because she felt she didn't need to attend his celebration. She thought because she held a great and grand position that she was all of that and a bag of chips. She allowed her ego to dictate to her demise. As a result, she was dethroned from a high and honorable position and forced to live as a common woman.

Here is another woman that had the attributes of a drama queen. Her name is Delilah. She was very manipulative and deceitful. She used her charm and wit to bring down a mighty and well-known man of God by the name of Samson. She used her slick words to get crucial information about Samson's guarded secret. After she began to stroke his ego, she assumed the upper hand advantage. It was a setup to cause Samson to be overtaken by his enemies. Samson was captured and overtaken by his enemies all because of a drama queen who knew his weakness. Samson suffered. He had his eyes put out. He was put in prison. He became prey to a drama queen. He eventually died because he got caught up in the web she used to entrap him. I would go on to say his destiny was cut short because he disobeyed his mother; she admonished Samson not to partake in Philistine women. But her beauty and charm lured him into a horrible state and cost him his future.

You can know a drama queen by these characteristics taking place in their lives. They never mind their own business, they are always in someone else's lane, and they will overstep boundaries, they have no limits and are not aware that they do these things. Self-love is a stabilizing validation drama queens don't understand. They have to have attention time and time again. Please beware that they come across as being very needy. They will say things like no one loves me, but are totally dependent upon others. They always seem to feel rejected or abandoned in some kind of way. It is a childish act that they used when they were children by playing the role of a victim. It got them the attention that they wanted then and now that they are an adult they will continue to use this type of behavior as a get over on others.

KIMBERLY'S PERSPECTIVE

Every day we must go before the Lord and allow Him to purge us of things that are not of Him. We must pray Psalm 51:10 that a pure heart is created in us. If we don't, we will stay in bondage and be used as a vessel of the enemy. Don't reject the flaws that the Holy Spirit reveals in you. They are being surfaced so you can deal with them and allow God to do a great work in you. If you want God's best, then take heed to the following identifiers, confess if you have them in your life, repent, and yield to God. God desires for us to mature so we can demonstrate Jesus Christ upon the Earth. We are ambassadors of Christ (2 Corinthians 5:20). Yet, if you have the following traits, then God's power is available to deliver you so people can see Jesus in you.

1. Selfish

Years ago, I was very selfish and I felt like the world revolved around me. As long as my needs were met, then I wasn't concerned about anyone else. It took me hitting rock bottom for me to realize my selfishness. Then, as I yielded my life to Jesus, I became a servant. Serving others helped me overcome selfishness. So, Jesus was a servant and He washed his disciple's feet.

Are you selfish? Do you only care about your needs? Do you lack compassion? Do you pray for others? Do you want others to succeed? Do you have the heart of God?

These questions will help you to identify if you are selfish. Ask God to give you a love for people.

2. Pride

Sometimes when the power of God flows through you in extraordinary ways, pride can set in. If you recognize it, then it must be dealt with immediately. To keep humble, I fall on my knees or praise God right after ministering. Every time a miracle occurs, I make sure God gets the glory and I don't even look for recognition. Don't get caught up in being acknowledged.

Allow God to promote you and let people boast on you. Never brag upon yourself.

Proverbs 27:2 (ESV) says, "Let another praise you, and not your own mouth; a stranger, and not your own lips."

Do you get offended when people don't mention you or when you don't get credit? Do you want to be the only one in the spotlight? Does it bother you when others are being promoted? Do you feel like you are the best?

If you answered yes to these questions, then pride is the culprit.

3. Jealous

Years ago, I would act out if I was jealous of someone. I made sure that the person knew that I didn't like them. I would compete with them so they wouldn't get what I wanted. If I saw a pretty girl, I would try to take the attention off her and place it upon myself. I did this by showing more skin or wearing fancy clothes. When I got saved, God showed me my insecurities. He built up my self-esteem and self-worth. We are all in the body of Christ and we need one another. We need to work together because we are a team.

1 Corinthians 12:1 says, "For as the body is one, and hath many members, and all the members of that one body, being many, are one body: so also is Christ."

Ask yourself the real reason why you don't like a particular individual? Are you uncomfortable if they outgrow you or go further than you? Are you threatened or intimidated by another's success? Do you feel like they will replace you?

These answers to these questions may be hard to swallow, but they will get to the root of the issue. So support and pray for the person you are jealous of and watch God place a love in your heart for them.

4. Hot-tempered

I used to make a big scene when I couldn't have my way. I would yell, pout, throw stuff, get attitudes with strangers, and put my business on blast on social media. Unfortunately, I didn't realize that I was being foolish and hurting my own reputation. As a result, I got arrested and ended up on probation for three years. Those years were a turning point in my life and God began to purge me of anger, hurt, abandonment, perversion, and other things. I learned the hard way to allow God to fight my battles. I had to be still and trust Him for vindication.

Do you go from zero to one hundred in a matter of seconds? Do you like to make a scene to embarrass the person who hurt you? Do you pray that others will fail? Do you think of ways to get revenge?

Be honest about those questions. Face your demons so they can be cast out. Yield the anger to God and instead of taking matters out in the natural, take them out in the spirit through prayer. Don't give the enemy the satisfaction of a reaction. Recognize that you are dealing with a spirit and not people. Respond how Jesus would in every situation.

Ephesians 6:12-13

12 For we wrestle not against flesh and blood, but against principalities, against powers, against the rulers of the darkness of this world, against spiritual wickedness in high places. 13 Wherefore take unto you the whole armour of God, that ye may be able to withstand in the evil day, and having done all, to stand.

CHAPTER 3

THE PERSONALITY DISORDER: SYMPTOMS OF A DRAMA QUEEN

CLAUDETTE'S PERSPECTIVE

A drama queen's life is filled with a rollercoaster of emotions. They start out wonderfully in relationships, but it turns out to be dreadful. They will readily storm out of a job if things are not going their way. They have to be the attention seeker in every situation. If you're always at the center of drama, here's a question you should ask yourself: What did I do to create this situation? Before you answer that, you are not doing anything and these dramatic situations just happen to you. If you have a history of constantly being involved in dramas, you're very likely playing an active role in creating that situation.

Whoever hates disguises himself with his lips and harbors deceit in his heart (Proverbs 26:24).

A drama queen secretly hates on others. Being a drama queen does not just show up in the way we talk. The root of the problem stems from the heart. If you are someone that has bitterness, anger, resentment and even hatred will eventually come up as a conflict. We need hearts that are slow to anger and quick to forgive. Only Jesus Christ can give that kind of heart transplant.

A lying tongue hates its victims and a flattering mouth works ruin (Proverbs 26:28). We have heard the old saying, "What a tangled web we weave when first we practice to deceive." Lying has a way of making a web of drama and struggle. Lying will eventually cause hurt feelings, ruin trust, and strained relationships. If you want to avoid being a drama queen, refuse to lie...even little white lies. Acknowledge that lying will cause ruin in your relationships. A drama queen is a woman who makes issues and problems about herself. Drama surrounds a Christian drama queen.

The First King of Israel, Saul was a king of great promise. But eventually the struggle with depression and anger due to his circumstances caused him to exhibit personality symptoms. I am not diagnosing anyone, but just like King Saul, if not handled properly your circumstances can have you act out of character and therefore, display symptoms of a Christian drama queen {I Samuel 16:14-23}. Let's take a closer look at King Saul's behavior.

In 1 Samuel 18, when David and Jonathan became friends, Saul became jealous of their friendship. Shortly after Saul appointed David as commander of his army. David went to battle; he fought against the Philistines and won. The women in Israel came out to meet King Saul with singing and dancing, saying, "Saul killed his thousands and David his ten thousands." And Saul became mad from then on he kept a jealous eye on David. An evil spirit came upon Saul, and he raved in his house like a madman to the point that he threw a javelin at David, but David escaped Saul twice. Saul saw how the Lord was with David and this made him insecure and afraid of David.

KIMBERLY'S PERSPECTIVE

Many Christian Drama queens don't have a handle on their emotions. They are on an emotional roller coaster. When things don't go their way, they automatically start making assumptions without having all the facts. I used to make assumptions and held hatred in my heart towards people that genuinely cared for me. Finally, I went to God and surrendered these feelings because I knew my heart was wicked. God instructed me to pray for the person I was jealous of several times throughout the day and be a blessing in their life. I eventually overcame my insecurities and embraced what God was doing in their life.

Jeremiah 17:9 says, "The heart is deceitful above all things, and desperately wicked: who can know it?"

Also, Christian drama queens feel like everyone is against them and deal with rejection often. When I feel hated, I get in God's presence so that He can heal the pain in my heart. We must realize that rejection is God's protection. Jesus understands everything that we go through. He is our high priest.

Hebrews 4:14-16
14 Seeing then that we have a great high priest, that is passed into the heavens, Jesus the Son of God, let us hold fast our profession.
15 For we have not a high priest which cannot be touched with the feeling of our infirmities; but was in all points tempted like as we are, yet without sin.

16 Let us therefore come boldly unto the throne of grace, that we may obtain mercy, and find grace to help in time of need.

The Israelites often rejected God. They committed spiritual adultery by serving other gods. The world doesn't revolve around us. There will always be someone that can do what we can better than us. There is always someone who may be more attractive or anointed than us. We must become comfortable in our own skin. We must embrace other's gifts. Especially those God sent to be a blessing in our lives. Some have hurt and destroyed those relationships that God sent to help them on this journey. Just because we have our insecurities, we must not take them out upon others. People don't deserve that. If you continue snapping at people or mistreating them, then you will end up alone. One day, you might not have anyone around because you have pushed them away.

There has been so much division in the body of Christ due to the Christian drama queen spirit. People are preaching a different Gospel. They say if you don't agree with them on political matters, then you aren't saved. If you don't speak in tongues, you are going to hell. If you don't operate in the supernatural, then you aren't a real Christian. If you look different or have a different preaching style, then you don't belong in this church. Sayings or beliefs like these have damaged the body. If we believe in our hearts and confess Jesus, then we are saved.

Romans 10:9 says, "That if thou shalt confess with thy mouth the Lord Jesus, and shalt believe in thine heart that God hath raised him from the dead, thou shalt be saved."

Stop making up your own traditions or laws. Jesus came to break the law and He shunned the traditions of men (Luke 13:10-17). Once we die to ourselves, God can increase in us and we can get delivered from the symptoms of being a Christian drama queen.

CHAPTER 4

DO MEN POSSESS THE DRAMA QUEEN MINDSET? ARE DRAMA QUEENS ONLY ONE GENDER?

CLAUDETTE'S PERSPECTIVE

I have found that this mentality really doesn't have a gender. I want you to take note that men can exhibit characteristics of Christian drama queens as well. We all know people who are constantly involved in drama. Drama queens are most likely described as a type of person. This type is equally applicable to men as well as women.

A drama queen can be anyone. Drama has no respect for people. A man can show visible signs of being full of drama. They display strong emotions, they use seduction, bullying and blaming to manipulate. Even males have constant confusion that they carry; they have the tendency to blame you for it. Male drama queens are drama addicts at any cost. Most people believe that women carry the most drama, however, it is often missed or overlooked in men. The male drama queen seeks conflict to create opportunities for violence or any negativity. Some violence created by male drama is physical even verbal and emotional; therefore, it is looked at as passive aggressive. They use the blame game often and do not like to be held accountable for responsibility. They will use having a bad upbringing as an excuse to be filled with drama. Word to the wise watch out for men who have nothing good to say about their family or anyone.

Male drama queen is full of hot air- all bark and no bite. They have potential but no performance. Now let's be clear about the male drama queen: They are very attractive, handsome and they have the tendency to suck the life out of you. They are counting on you to invite them in. Ladies, be sure you have self-love and self- preservation to see the tactics and lies of a male drama queen before you allow him access to your home, money, body and heart. Don't go by appearance, go by behavior as time goes by. A drama male queen is the exact opposite of a grown man.

KIMBERLY'S PERSPECTIVE

In the Body of Christ, there is neither Greek nor Jew, male nor female.

Galatians 3:28 says, "There is neither Jew nor Greek, there is neither bond nor free, there is neither male nor female: for ye are all one in Christ Jesus."

Men can be Christian drama queens as well. For instance, many people always associate Jezebel with a woman but fail to realize that men have this spirit. Men can become selfish, jealous, angry, prideful, hot-tempered, and carnal. Let's look at some men in the Bible who had the 'Christian Drama Queen' spirit.

1. Nabal

Nabal's name means fool and he did some foolish things. He was very selfish even though he had enough food to share with others. He was very harsh and mistreated others around him. He was very self-centered and lacked compassion. One day, King David sent messengers to Nabal to get some food. They had always protected Nabal's vineyard and they wanted to see if he would be kind enough to return the favor. However, these messengers were met with a rude response. King David became upset and was ready to kill Nabal and his whole household. Nabal's wife Abigail immediately went to action by gathering up some supplies and offered them to King David and his men. She knew what kind of man she was married to. Her swift actions saved Nabal's servants' life. Unfortunately, Nabal couldn't handle others being blessed, so when he found out what had happened, he died. Being a Christian drama queen can kill us prematurely.

2. Gehazi

Gehazi was greedy and he went behind his master's back. So he didn't get to receive the double portion anointing that his mentor Elisha had received from his mentor Elijah. Gehazi didn't have great character and was only concerned about his own gain. One day, Naaman, a great leader, had become stricken with leprosy. He heard how God was using Elisha and came for healing. He was instructed to dip in the dirty Jordan river seven times. He didn't want to at first but was desperate for a miracle. When he became miraculously healed, he wanted to bless Elisha, but the prophet refused. So Gehazi goes chasing after Naaman to get these gifts and when Elisha found out, leprosy came upon him. The 'Christian Drama

Queen' spirit can open up a demonic portal in our lives and cause sickness.

3. Saul

Saul couldn't handle someone else getting more credit than him. One day after the war, the women began to sing, "Saul has killed his thousands and David has killed his ten thousand. (1 Samuel 18:7)." When Saul heard that, he hated David. David was faithful to Saul and loved him very much. However, that didn't matter to Saul and he tried to kill David at least 12 times.

In 1 Samuel 18 and 19 we see the following:

1 Samuel 18:11, Saul throws his spear at David twice.

In 1 Samuel 18:13, Saul makes David commander of 1,000, hoping he will be killed.

In 1 Samuel 18:17, Merab is offered to David, if he fights the Lord's battles like a valiant man, he thought that he wouldn't have to kill him because the Philistines would do that. However when the time came to marry, Saul gave him to someone else. Saul was a liar and Indian giver.

In 1 Samuel 18:20, Michal is offered to David for 100 Philistine foreskins, and he presents 200. He wanted his daughter to become a trap for him.

In 1 Samuel 19:1, Saul orders Jonathan and his servants to kill David, but Jonathan warns David. Jonathan talked with his father and told him that David was innocent. Saul lied and said, "David will not be put to death," so David returned.

In 1 Samuel 19:10, Saul slings his spear at David again after a battle.

In 1 Samuel 19:11, David fled to his house and Saul sent messengers to David's house to watch it and kill him, but Michal warned David.

In 1 Samuel 19:18, Saul sends three groups of men to Naioth (where the prophets were prophesying) to take David, then comes himself.

Eventually, Saul reaps what he had sown. He ended dying in battle by committing suicide (1 Samuel 31). He had sent David to battle many times, hoping that he would be killed. Be careful being a Christian drama queen. God is not mocked. One reaps what they have sown.

Galatians 6:7 says, "Be not deceived; God is not mocked: for whatsoever a man soweth, that shall he also reap."

CHAPTER 5

HOW TO DEAL WITH A DRAMA QUEEN?

CLAUDETTE'S PERSPECTIVE

To defuse the behavior or attributes of a drama queen means to simply set clear boundaries, make sure that you let them know that you will not be sucked into their web of confusion and chaos. Disappoint them by eliminating their power of attention seeking. Tell the victim that there are things you will and will not tolerate from them. Keep your conversation with them in the positive direction; refuse to participate in anything that will cause manipulation or out right trouble. Even if the drama queen feels as if you are being harsh, that is your opportunity to put some space between you two. Remember you aren't anyone's trash can and you should not feel as if it is your duty to play the role of caring for a drama queen in the event that it causes you to be weighed down by unnecessary junk.

When it comes to dealing with a drama queen you may want to take into consideration that the individual may have some mental issues. Even if they are dealing with mental issues it is not your place to try and fix them. It is ok to walk away from someone who may be causing you stress. Let them know the reason for walking away from them. Also, suggest to the individual that they may need counseling or therapy.

Proverbs 26:20 Drama is like a fire. It dies out when you stop feeding it so stop talking on and on about it. Don't pick at it over lunch or text about it into the night. Especially when you are not directly involved in the conflict, you don't need to know the details and updates.

KIMBERLY'S PERSPECTIVE

Christian Drama Queens may be difficult to deal with but not impossible. It may be impossible with man but not impossible with God (Matthew 19:26). We can pray for them and love them from a distance. However, when we interact with them, we need the wisdom of God. God will give us strategies to overcome these challenges and hopefully, the person may recognize the error of their ways and get delivered. Deliverance is the children's bread (Matthew 15:26-28).

First, we must pray for those who are 'Christian Drama Queens'. Prayer changes things. We must recognize that we can't change anyone, but only God can. He can take the heart of stone and put in a heart of flesh.

Ezekiel 11:19 (ESV) says, "And I will give them one heart, and a new spirit I will put within them. I will remove the heart of stone from their flesh and give them a heart of flesh."

The king's heart is in God's hands.

Proverbs 21:1 says, "The king's heart is in the hand of the Lord, as the rivers of water: he turneth it whithersoever he will."

God can demote and promote others. So as we pray and stand in the gap for others, God is moving behind the scenes. Some of these people's lives depend on our prayers. They might not know how bound they are. Our prayers will break demonic strongholds and cause spiritual cataracts to fall off their eyes. No matter how nasty they may be to us, we must pray for our enemies. We bless those who try to curse us.

Don't pray that something bad would happen to them but pray that God's will be done in their lives and that they will prosper. Pray for them as you would yourself.

Matthew 5:44 says, "But I say unto you, Love your enemies, bless them that curse you, do good to them that hate you, and pray for them which despitefully use you, and persecute you;"

You may not feel like praying for them, but it's your duty as a true believer in Jesus. Even if they persecute us, we still have to pray for them. Also, forgive them because they know not what they are doing. Jesus prayed for His crucifiers (Luke 23:34).

Next, you want to love them from a distance. God tells us to guard our hearts because out of it flows the issues of life (Proverbs 4:23). You must use wisdom. You may genuinely care about this individual, but their actions continue to hurt you. Recognize that you are dealing with a spirit and cut off some access. Put boundaries in place. When they call your phone, it's okay not to answer. When they message you on social media, you don't have to respond. If they knock on your door, you don't have to answer. You aren't a doormat or someone's punching bag. You must distance yourself for your own sanity and your healing. While there is space between you and the individual who is a drama queen, still pray for them. Still respond in love or demonstrate God's compassion during any interaction. When your enemy is hungry, give them something to eat. When they are thirsty, give them something to drink. As a result, you are reaping hot coals upon their head.

Proverbs 25:21-22 says, "If thine enemy be hungry, give him bread to eat; and if he be thirsty, give him water to drink: 22 For thou shalt heap coals of fire upon his head, and the Lord shall reward thee."

Lastly, you need God's wisdom when dealing with Christian drama queens. You must make sure you respond accordingly, especially if you are caught off guard. You must walk circumspectly as the wise, not as the foolish (Ephesians 5:15). So everything that you do, God's wisdom must be applied. If you lack wisdom, cry out to God and He will give it to you generously (James 1:5). God will even give you another measure of wisdom called sound wisdom (Proverbs 2:7). You are actually putting safety nets in place so the enemy can't get you in your flesh. The devil wants you to go off on these individuals. If you take the bait, you are hurting your witness for the Lord Jesus Christ. How can you win them over if you are just as rude and nasty?

CHAPTER 6

THE COMMONALITIES OF DRAMA QUEENS AND NARCISSISTS

CLAUDETTE'S PERSPECTIVE

A narcissist is a person who has an excessive interest in or admiration of themselves. In other words they think the world revolves around them. This is a disorder in which a person has an inflated sense of self-importance.

A drama queen is a person who habitually responds to situations in a melodramatic way. This is a person who often has exaggerated or overly emotional reactions to events or situations.

Most narcissists cannot handle things going smoothly for a long period of time. If everything is going in a uniform manner a narcissist cannot tolerate it. They are easily bored, since they do not have control over their own minds or themselves, they have to have control over people or things. They will do anything to get their own needs met. The key factor with narcissists is that they thrive off of drama and dividing others. They love to bully others then they hide themselves as being the one who created the drama. They are sometimes called Narcs. They love conflict, they love to make you cry, they control you none of it is good, it is very toxic and nasty. If you are connected to a narcissist you will never have a peaceful life. They see situations through a different eye lens therefore, making everything about them. They are often complainers who love to have attention, attention, attention even in public they act out to get their way.

Drama queens and narcissists share some of the same attributes. They both put on great shows. but it is not real. Basically nothing is real about them. It is almost like a catfish situation where you don't know what you are dealing with until it is too late. Drama is an attention seeking tactic that narcissists will use to lie and then convert it into a dramatic story.

KIMBERLY'S PERSPECTIVE

Everyone knows that a narcissist is difficult to deal with and most relationships end up in divorce or strained. A 'Christian Drama Queen' and a narcissist have a few things in common. We will explore each one.

1. An inflated sense of importance

Both feel like they are the best and no one can outdo them. They toot their own horn and often boast about their own accomplishments. You will often see them name-drop or mention notable people to make themselves seem more important. They are always trying to impress others because there is an ulterior motive. Perhaps they want to be on certain platforms, so they try to puff themselves up to the leader of the ministry. Maybe they want to walk through certain doors, so they exaggerate their qualifications. Their tongues are flattering and they will compliment you just to get what they want. They have a serpent's tongue (Psalm 140:3). Don't take the bait of flattery. They can say the right words but beware. Pay attention to the red flags. Listen to the Holy Spirit. Use discernment. If the alarms are going off in your spirit, take heed.

2. A deep need for excessive attention and admiration

Christian drama queens and narcissists need the spotlight to feed their egos. If they sense someone up and coming, they become threatened and may try to block their promotion. They may try to close doors for others by planting lies. They will try to turn others against them for no legit reason. Christian drama queens and narcissists don't believe in passing the baton or equipping the next generation. The only people that are anointing in their ministries are them. They need everyone to worship or bow at their feet. If the people's lives aren't about them, then that's a problem. Christian drama queens and narcissists have made themselves gods in people's lives. Whenever someone wants glory instead of giving it to Jesus, run. Whenever someone misuses the term honor, run. Honoring someone isn't always about publicly announcing it on social media. It is what you do when a crowd isn't around. It is also how you respond during interaction. Lastly, honor is a heart posture towards an individual. However, Christian drama queens and narcissists abuse this term and place unrealistic demands on others that keep them in bondage or submission.

3. Lack of empathy for others

Christian drama queens and narcissists aren't concerned about what God wants to do or His plans. Their only concern is about themselves. They want to be famous and don't care who they hurt to get to the top. They want money and don't care who they cheat or manipulate to accumulate wealth. They want power and aren't concerned about abusing it once it's obtained. They don't care anything about serving others and everything it's about, "What will I get out of it?" They don't sacrifice so God can be glorified. They forgot where they started from or their humble beginnings. They weren't always wealthy or in demand. They won't preach at smaller churches because the honorarium is too small. Sometimes, God wants us to be a blessing to those who can't afford it. We must give alms and bless the less fortunate. When we give unto the poor, we are lending to God (Proverbs 19:17). Don't turn your nose upon those who are struggling. We weren't always saints. Just a few years ago, most of us were in prostitution, fornication, alcoholism, jail, or lack in some manner. Don't judge because the same measure you judge others, you will reap that same standard.

Matthew 7:2 says, "For with the judgment you pronounce you will be judged, and with the measure you use it will be measured to you."

4. Often having troubled relationships

Christian drama queens and narcissists have troubled relationships. They may start off sweet, especially during the courtship phase. However, during the marriage, Mr. Jekyll and Mr. Hyde will come out. You will feel like you are married to a stranger or sleeping with the enemy. Christian drama queens and narcissists feel like they have you now, so they don't have to be on their best behavior. As a result, they will treat you in any kind of way, even crossing healthy boundaries, because they feel like you won't leave them. Due to their selfish behaviors, they don't consider your feelings and think, "Oh, they will get over it." They will even say harmful things, not realizing that it eventually affects your soul. Words hurt and tear you down. Over time, you begin to lose yourself in the relationship and become unhappy. It will take God's delivering power to bring you out or to set your partner free. Also, many covenants are broken due to Christian drama queens and narcissists. People are leaving ministries left and right because they are hurting each other. If you are going through church hurt, don't turn your back on God. People hurt you, not God. God loves you so much. We must stop putting people on pedestals and realize that they are flesh, just like us. The sick need the doctor or the sick go to the hospital (Matthew 9:12).

CHAPTER 7

HOW WILL CHRISTIAN DRAMA QUEENS CONTROL YOU?

CLAUDETTE'S PERSPECTIVE

A drama queen loves the spotlight. Once they have it they feel as if no one else is entitled to all the attention and no one else matters. Anything you have going on doesn't matter to them, it is unimportant. In their minds everything is about them they will use the smallest comment or action and make it their own personal story. When they make everything personal, you are always viewed as second place to them. When a normal individual views something minor or just shrugs it off, the drama queen will take it and blow it out of proportion to them. It has to be catastrophic. They intentionally stir up situations and make confusion just to allow them to shine. One of the biggest attributes about a drama queen that assures their control is they love to gossip about others. Gossip is a tactic they use to control others. They feel the need to be busy with other people's business. Criticizing comes as second nature to drama queens. They love to fuss about everything. If you are in a relationship like this or heading in that direction, please run. Your life will be much better.

KIMBERLY'S PERSPECTIVE

Christian drama queens want to have their way and will stop at no cost. They will do the following to control your life:

1. Restrict access to money

Years ago, there was a prophet in the body of Christ that stumbled. He was a Christian drama queen. He competed against many by trying to out preach and prophesy them. When he would travel, he met various ladies in different cities. He was a married man but his actions while away didn't reflect that. When he first met his wife, he swept her off her feet by making empty promises. Once married, he used money to control her. He didn't want her to get her hair because he didn't want people to look at his wife. He didn't want her to leave the house to get her nails done because he was afraid that she would leave him for someone else. He would hide the car keys so she couldn't go anywhere. If he was away preaching, he would cut her credit cards off or move the money out of the accounts so she couldn't have any gas money. His fear was disillusioned. Their marriage eventually fell apart due to controlling behavior and extramarital affairs. A huge scandal broke out and they divorced. The prophet is no longer preaching. Their failed marriage hurt many people. However, as the young prophet seeks God, he can be restored and delivered.

2. Buy you or have you name that price

Christian Drama queens will try to buy you as a tool to control you. We must not be desperate even if we need the money. We must turn down some opportunities and trust God. Every opportunity or door isn't from God. It could be a counterfeit or demonic gateway to suck you in, so your ministry or destiny is destroyed. We have been bought with the blood of Jesus. We have been bought with a price.

1 Corinthians 6:19-20 (ESV) says, "Or do you not know that your body is a temple of the Holy Spirit within you, whom you have from God? You are not your own, for you were bought with a price. So glorify God in your body."

If someone can buy you, then they can control what you do or preach. If someone says, "I'll give you one thousand dollars if you don't preach against sin," politely decline.

In Genesis 30:28, Laban tried to buy Jacob when his season with him was up. If Jacob would've stayed, then he would have continued to be taking advantage of and missed out on the promise that God had for him.

3. Withhold intimacy (if married)

Christian drama queens will use sex as a weapon. God created sex to be enjoyed between married couples who are a man and a woman. He never intended sex to be used as a manipulation tool. "If you don't do what I say or want, then I will not have sex with you." God tells us not to withhold sex from our spouses. Men need sex and often desire it more than women. Why allow the enemy to come in by being petty? Even if you don't feel like having sex, do it as an act of service unto your spouse. The only time sex should be withheld is for a time of prayer and fasting that has to be agreed upon by both parties.

1 Corinthians 7:5 (NKJV) says, "Do not deprive one another except with consent for a time, that you may give yourselves to fasting and prayer; and come

together again so that Satan does not tempt you because of your lack of self-control."

4. Ignore you

Christian Drama Queens will ignore you as a way to hurt you because they hurt. They enjoy giving others the silent treatment. They will treat you like a stranger or roommate if you live with them. They will lie to themselves and say, "This person is dead to me." Not communicating with your loved ones hurts. God desires communication even with us. He always longed to fellowship with mankind. He wanted to visit his people on Mount Sinai, but they were too afraid (Exodus 20). They felt like they were going to die if they saw God in the fire. It is impossible to have a relationship if there is no communication.

5. Conspire against you

Christian drama queens will conspire against you. They will blatantly lie in your face or make false deals with you just to control you. For instance, in Genesis 30, Laban asked Jacob what he wanted. Jacob said that he wanted the speckled, spotted, and streaked goats. However, Laban did the opposite. He told his servant to take all the speckled, spotted, and streaked goats far away so Jacob couldn't find them. His servant took the goats a distance that was three days away. Laban felt that Jacob would never leave because the goats that he wanted weren't present.

CHAPTER 8

HOW TO GET FREE FROM A DRAMA QUEEN MENTALITY?

CLAUDETTE'S PERSPECTIVE

Are you a drama magnet? To be honest, no one really wants to admit that they may be a drama queen or a magnet for drama. But really, are you? Does your life always have drama? Here are some ways to know if you are a drama queen or a drama magnet.

Personalize things that aren't personal
Always want to control things that you really can't
Obsession with your appearance
Stirring up drama
Fascination with drama
Always in arguments with others

You get a thrill out of airing your or someone else dirty laundry out on social media.

Do any of these describe you? If any of these attributes describe you, Would you be willing to remove the drama out of your life? Let's look at the Word of God to see how Apostle Paul teaches his mentee Timothy how to discern and avoid drama in the church. When Apostle Paul met Timothy, he asked him to join him in spreading the good news of Jesus Christ. They begin their journey across the Roman Empire carrying the message of the good news of Jesus Christ. But as time went on, Paul appointed Timothy as pastor of the church of Ephesus. There was trouble in the church, so Paul wrote a letter to Timothy to beware of drama magnets and drama queens. As we look at 1 Timothy 3-11, Paul had a command for Timothy. He stated that he has been hearing about the drama queens in the church and Timothy must stop them. This may sound a bit firm, but understand that Paul started this church. So he knew the character of the people in the Ephesus's church. Paul spent three years in the church of Ephesus. In the letter, Paul reminds Timothy that the people there need a pure heart, a good conscience, and sincere faith, leading them to love. So what Paul was really saying was that a transformation was needed because what's on the inside is very important. Paul then teaches Timothy a very powerful principle about faith. Disciples of Jesus Christ stop the drama because they have been transformed inwardly. Disciples of Jesus Christ have a pure heart, clear conscience, and sincere faith. All of these attributes work together to build a solid foundation of love in our lives. It is a foundation that cannot be shaken by drama or controversy.

So, how do we change from the inside? How do we transform an unforgiving heart into a pure heart? How do we change a bad conscience into a pure conscience? How do we change weak faith into strong faith?

1. Pray that God will change you. Spend more time in prayer. Go deeper in prayer.
2. Study the Word of God. Are you reading the Bible daily?
3. Be accountable. Are you talking about your life with someone you can trust? Just like Paul was staying in touch with Timothy through letters, we need people in our lives to help us grow.

KIMBERLY'S PERSPECTIVE

If you are a Christian drama queen, there is hope for you. God's power can set you free but you must want deliverance. Let's look at 2 Chronicles 7:14 and follow the steps for deliverance. If you apply what the Scripture says, then God will hear your prayers, forgive, and heal your land by making you whole.

If my people, which are called by my name, shall humble themselves, and pray, and seek my face, and turn from their wicked ways; then will I hear from heaven, and will forgive their sin, and will heal their land.

1) Humble yourself

Sometimes we have to get to the end of ourselves and recognize the need for God in our lives. Eventually, we will get tired of doing things in our own strength and must rely on Him. The best way to humble yourself is by fasting. When we fast, we are humbling our souls. Point people to Jesus and never yourself. Stay hidden in Jesus and become a servant. Pride comes before destruction—a haughty look before a fall (Proverbs 16:18). God opposes the proud but gives grace unto the humble (James 4:6).

2) Pray and seek God's face.

If you haven't been intimate with God in a while, then prayer may be difficult. You can say a prayer from your heart. When we seek God with our whole heart, we will find Him. Seek the Lord while He is near.

Isaiah 55:6-7 says, "6 Seek ye the Lord while he may be found, call ye upon him while he is near: 7 Let the wicked forsake his way, and the unrighteous man his thoughts: and let him return unto the Lord, and he will have mercy upon him; and to our God, for he will abundantly pardon."

Tell God the truth. Confess your sins. It's time to stop repetitious prayers. Jesus rebuked the Sadducees and Pharisees for the long fancy prayers. Learn how to be naked and ashamed in front of God. In other words, be yourself. He is your Creator. Once in prayer, stay there until the Lord releases you. Don't rush your time with God. Allow His refining fire to purge out anything not like Him. Pray for a burden of prayer and intercession. Once in prayer, seek God for His counsel and His will to be done in your life.

3) Turn from wicked ways.

Repent in prayer and stop doing these harmful things. Repenting is a turning away from sin or a behavior change. As far as the east is from the west, so are your transgressions removed from God (Psalm 103:12). He will throw your sins into the sea of forgetfulness (Micah 7:19). Now that God has forgiven you for all the evil things that you have done, forgive yourself. Don't allow the enemy to cause condemnation. Remember, there is no condemnation in Christ, but you must walk in the spirit (Romans 8:1). You have to follow after the Holy Spirit by allowing Him to guide you. Let God order your steps.

Wholeness is another level than healing. Healing can be superficial or alleviate symptoms of an ailment, but wholeness can penetrate the soul. Some other attributes of Christian drama queens came from deep-rooted issues in the soul. In Luke 17:11-19, only one leper out of ten returned to Jesus after he was healed. As a result, he was made whole. Cry out and surrender to God today. Victor is your portion. You are a new creature in Christ. The old man has passed away (2 Corinthians 5:17). As you yield to God, He will bless you with new beginnings.

ABOUT THE AUTHORS

CLAUDETTE DIXON WILSON

The Prophet. The Teacher. The Vessel. Operating in the Five-Fold Ministry Internationally to build the Kingdom of God through the preaching and teaching of the Word. From the laying on of hands and prophesying to preaching and teaching the unadulterated truth, Apostle Claudette Wilson is an anointed and powerful vessel of God. With her supernatural delivery and holy boldness, she keeps audiences captivated and engaged as she imparts wisdom and knowledge for daily walking with God. Her realness is only surpassed by her strong desire to see the people of God delivered and healed for real.

Apostle Wilson is a Southern Belle, from Foley, Alabama. Her roots in the Word and things of God run deep. She has an affinity for the people of God. She wishes above all things to see people prosper and be in health, just as His word says. She has founded many churches across the globe to ensure people have a place to go and hear the Word and assemble themselves together corporately. With over two decades of service to God, Apostle Wilson is on the wall and she is not coming down. She travels nationally and internationally preaching and teaching to people of all ages, cultures, backgrounds and nationalities. As Overseer of International Eagles Fellowship Outreach, Inc., she oversees ministries and churches around the world. Apostle Wilson is a Mother, Mentor and Motivational Speaker to say the least. She undergirds the nonprofit organization H.U.S.H. (Healing Under Strategic Help), where people are being healed for real and C.H.A.M.P., a mentoring program for ages 12-30 to impact and change the lives of the next generation. Outreach always has and always will be Apostle Wilson's passion. She ministers at revivals, retreats, conferences, on television (including TBN), radio and any platform God has assigned her to. She is not afraid to go into the trenches and low places that others are not willing to go. Wherever the Lord sends her, she is willing and obedient to carry out His will.

Apostle Wilson received her Doctorate degree in leadership, Counseling and Business from Higher

Place Christian University in Dallas, Texas. She is an astute student of the word of God and an excellent leader and counselor which is evident immediately upon hearing her speak. She is a Spiritual Advisor for the New South Fulton Council Capitol Atlanta District 7. She is entrusted with the souls of many throughout the nations. God has called her to be a gamechanger and that is exactly who she is.

Anointed and appointed, chosen from amongst the ones who were counted out. God found her faithful over a few things and has raised her up to make her ruler over much. Sought after by many, she has become a spiritual mother and covering to those who were broken and on the verge of giving up. She has a special gift of making people believe they can do anything and causing them to make a complete turnaround in their lives.

Beautiful and radiant, inside and out, the light of hope and love shines bright on this woman of God. She is truly a crown jewel and a blessing to the Kingdom of God. An upright, strong, courageous Christian warrior on the battlefield for the Lord. She is Kingdom minded operating in Kingdom principles. Above all, Apostle Wilson is a vessel of honor being used for God's glory in the earth. She is impacting and changing lives through truth and love and building the Kingdom daily.

KIMBERLY MOSES

Kimberly Moses started off her ministry as Kimberly Hargraves. She is highly sought after as a prophetic voice, intercessor and prolific author. There is no doubt that she has a global mandate on her life to serve the nations of the world by spreading the Gospel of Jesus Christ. She has a quickly expanding worldwide healing and deliverance ministry. Kimberly Moses wears many hats to fulfill the call God has placed on her life as an entrepreneur over several businesses including her own personal brand Rejoice Essentials which promotes the Gospel of Jesus Christ.

She also serves as a life coach and mentor to many women. She is also the loving mother of two wonderful children. She is married to Tron. Kimberly has dedicated her life to the work of ministry and to serve others under the call God has placed over her life. Kimberly currently resides in South Carolina.

She is a very anointed woman of God who signs, miracles and wonders follow. The miraculous and incessant testimonies attributed to her ministry are incalculable, with many reporting physical and mental healing, financial breakthroughs, debt cancellations and other favorable outcomes. She is known across the globe as a servant who truly labors on behalf of God's people through intercession.

She is the author of The Following:

"Overcoming Difficult Life Experiences with Scriptures and Prayers"
"Overcoming Emotions with Prayers"
"Daily Prayers That Bring Changes"
"In Right Standing,"
"Obedience Is Key,"
"Prayers That Break The Yoke Of The Enemy: A Book Of Declarations,"
"Prayers That Demolish Demonic Strongholds: A Book Of Declarations,"
"Work Smarter. Not Harder. A Book Of Declarations For The Workforce,"
"Set The Captives Free: A Book Of Deliverance."
"Pray More Challenge"
"Walk By Faith: A Daily Devotional"
"Empowering The New Me: Fifty Tips To Becoming A Godly Woman"

"School of the Prophets: A Curriculum For Success"
"8 Keys To Accessing The Supernatural"
"Conquering The Mind: A Daily Devotional"
"Enhancing The Prophetic In You"
"The ABCs of The Prophetic: Prophetic Characteristics"
"Wisdom Is The Principal Thing: A Daily Devotional"
"It Cost Me Everything"
"The Making Of A Prophet: Women Walking in Prophetic Destiny"
"The Art of Meditation: A Daily Devotional"
"Warfare Strategies: Biblical Weapons"
"Becoming A Better You"
"I Almost Died"
"The Pastor's Secret: The D.L. Series"
"June Bug The Busy Bee: The Gamer"
"June Bug The Busy Bee: The Bully"
"The Weary Prophet: Providing Practical Steps For Restoration"
"The Insignificant Woman"
"The Foolish Woman: A Daily Devotional"
"June Bug The Busy Bee: Sibling Rivalry"
"All Things Relationships"
"30 Day Pray For Your Spouse Challenge"

You can find more about Kimberly at
www.kimberlyhargraves.com

For Rejoice Essential Magazine, visit
www.rejoiceessential.com

For beauty and t-shirts, visit
www.rejoicingbeauty.com

Please write a review for my books on Amazon.com

Support this ministry:
Cashapp: $ProphetessKimberly
Paypal.me/remag
Venmo: Kimberly-Moses-19

INDEX

A

abandoned, 14
abandonment, 17
Abigail, 28
Academy Award, 5
accomplishments, 39
accountable, 26, 51
addicts, 26
admiration, 37, 40
admonished, 13
adultery, 8, 23
advantage, 13, 46
affection, 6
affinity, 56
afraid, 21, 45, 47, 56
ages, 56
Alabama, 55
alcoholism, 41
alms, 41

ambassadors, 14
anger, 9, 17, 18, 20, 21
angry, 27
anointed, 23, 55, 60
anointing, 28, 40
anxiety, 6
Apostle Claudette Dixon, 2
Apostle Dixon, 2
Apostle Paul, 50
appearance, 49
approval, 2, 5
arguments, 11, 49
arrested, 17
assumptions, 22
atmosphere, 2
attention, 5, 6, 11, 14, 16, 19, 32, 38, 39, 40, 43
attractive, 23, 26
attributes, 1, 13, 32, 38, 44, 50, 51, 54
author, 59, 60

B

backgrounds, 56
bad conscience, 51
bait, 36, 39
baton, 40
battle, 21, 30
battles, 9, 18, 29
Beautiful, 57

beauty, 13, 62
behavior, 6, 7, 14, 21, 27, 32, 42, 45, 53
benefits, 4
Bible, 12, 27, 51
bitterness, 20
blame, 26
blaming, 26
blocked, 10
blood, 18, 45
Body of Christ, 27
bondage, 14, 40
book, 1, 2
boundaries, 13, 32, 35, 42
broadcast, 2
broken, 42, 57
bully, 38
bullying, 26
business, 13, 17, 44

C

car keys, 45
carnal, 27
catastrophic, 43
celebration, 12
chaos, 11, 32
characteristics, 7, 13, 25
charm, 13
cheat, 41

childish act, 14
children, 12, 14, 34, 59
church, 9, 23, 42, 50
churches, 5, 41, 56
circumspectly, 36
clarity, 1
comfortable, 23
commander, 21, 29
Commonalities, 3, 37
communication, 47
compassion, 15, 27, 36
compliment, 39
condemnation, 54
confess, 14, 24
conflict, 20, 26, 33, 38
confusion, 26, 32
consent, 46
contractions, 2
control, 7, 10, 38, 44, 45, 46, 47, 49
Control, 3, 7, 43
controversy, 51
counseling, 33
Counseling, 56
counterfeit, 45
couples, 46
courageous, 57
courtship, 42
credit cards, 45
crowd, 40

cry, 36, 38
culprit, 16
cultures, 56
curse, 9, 34, 35

D

dancing, 21
David, 21, 27, 28, 29, 30
deceit, 20
deceitful, 13, 22
deceived, 31
deception, 11
Delilah, 13
deliverance, 51, 59
delivered, 24, 34, 45, 55
demonic gateway, 45
demonic strongholds, 34
demons, 18
demonstrate, 8, 14, 36
dependent, 14
depressed, 9
depression, 21
deprive, 46
desire, 46, 55
destiny, 1, 13, 45
destruction, 52
dethroned, 12
devout, 5

difficult, 33, 39, 52
direction, 44
dirty laundry, 50
Disappoint, 32
discernment, 39
disciple, 15
disobeyed, 13
Disorder, 3, 6, 19
disrespected, 12
dissatisfaction, 6
divorce, 39
drama, 1, 4, 5, 6, 7, 8, 9, 10, 11, 12, 13, 14, 19, 20, 21, 22, 23, 24, 25, 26, 27, 28, 30, 32, 33, 36, 37, 38, 40, 41, 42, 43, 44, 46, 47, 49, 50, 51, 54
drama queen, 1, 4, 5, 6, 9, 11, 12, 13, 19, 20, 21, 23, 24, 26, 28, 30, 32, 33, 36, 37, 43, 44, 49, 51
dramatic, 6, 7, 19, 38
dreadful, 19
drunkenness, 8

E

earth, 57
ego, 12, 13
Elisha, 28
embarrass, 18
embrace, 1, 23
emotional,, 7
emotions, 19, 21, 26

emulations, 8
enemies, 13, 34, 35
enemy, 12, 14, 18, 36, 42, 46, 54
entrap, 13
envious, 12
Envyings, 8
Ephesus, 50
events, 37
evil day, 18
evil spirit, 21
exaggerated, 37
excuses, 9
extramarital affairs, 45
eye, 21, 38
eyes, 9, 13, 34

F

fail, 18, 27
faith, 8, 50, 51
falsely accused, 12
family, 26
famous, 41
fancy clothes, 16
fasting, 46, 52
favor, 28
favorable, 60
fear, 45
feelings, 20, 22, 42

fellowship, 47
female, 27
fight, 7, 18
fire, 33, 36, 47, 53
flaws, 14
flesh, 8, 18, 34, 36, 42
fool, 9, 27
foolish, 17, 27, 36
forgive, 20, 35, 52, 53
fornication, 8, 41
foundation, 51
friendly, 8
friendship, 21
fruit, 8, 10
fuss, 44
future, 13

G

gas money, 45
Gehazi, 28
gender, 6, 25
Gender, 3, 25
generation, 40, 56
gentle, 9
gentleness, 8
gifts, 23, 28
glory, 2, 10, 15, 40, 57
goats, 47, 48

God, 2, 5, 8, 9, 12, 13, 14, 15, 16, 17, 18, 22, 23, 24, 28, 30, 31, 33, 34, 35, 36, 41, 42, 45, 46, 47, 50, 51, 52, 53, 54, 55, 56, 57, 59, 60
good conscience, 50
good news, 50
goodness, 8
Gospel, 23, 59
gossip, 9, 44
gossiping, 11
grace, 23, 52
Greek, 5, 27
guilty, 7

H

happy, 7
harsh, 27, 32
hated, 22, 29
hates, 20
hatred, 8, 20, 22
haughty, 52
healing, 28, 35, 54, 59, 60
health, 56
heart, 14, 15, 17, 20, 22, 24, 26, 34, 40, 50, 51, 52
hearts, 20, 24, 35
Heaven, 2
heavens, 22
heavy, 9
hell, 23

heresies, 8
high priest, 22
hills, 10
Hindrances, 4
holy boldness, 55
Holy Spirit, 1, 8, 14, 39, 45, 54
home, 6, 26
honest, 7, 18, 49
honor, 40, 57
honorable, 13
honorarium, 41
hope, 51, 57
horn, 39
horrible state, 13
hospital, 42
hot air, 26
hot coals, 36
Hot Topics, 2
Hot-tempered, 17
house, 21, 30, 44
household, 28
humble, 5, 15, 41, 52
hurt, 17, 18, 20, 23, 35, 41, 42, 45, 47
hurting, 17, 36, 42
husband, 12
hypocrite, 5

I

identifiers, 14
identity, 5
Idolatry, 8
Ignore, 47
illegal thoughts, 5
imitators, 7
impress, 39
Indian giver, 29
infirmities, 22
insecure, 21
insecurities, 16, 22, 23
instability, 6
instigators, 9
intercession, 53, 60
intimidated, 17
issues, 20, 33, 35, 54

J

Jacob, 12, 46, 47, 48
jail, 41
javelin, 21
jealous, 12, 16, 17, 21, 22, 27
Jealous, 16
Jesus, 10, 14, 15, 18, 20, 22, 24, 27, 35, 36, 40, 45, 50, 51, 52, 53, 54, 59
Jew, 27
jewel, 57
Jezebel, 12, 27

Jonathan, 21, 30
Jordan river, 28
journey, 23, 50
joy, 8, 9
judge, 41
judgment, 41
junk, 33

K

Kavod, 2
killed, 21, 29, 30
King Ahab, 12
kingdom of God, 8
knowledge, 1, 55

L

Laban, 46, 47, 48
labors, 60
ladies, 44
land, 52
lasciviousness, 8
law, 8, 24
leader, 28, 39, 57
Leah, 12
leper, 54
leprosy, 28
letters, 51

liar, 29
limits, 13
lips, 16, 20
lives, 13, 23, 29, 34, 35, 40, 51, 52, 56, 57, 58
longsuffering, 8
Lord, 2, 9, 14, 21, 24, 29, 34, 36, 52, 53, 56, 57
love, 6, 8, 9, 13, 15, 17, 26, 33, 35, 36, 38, 44, 50, 51, 57, 58
lunch, 33
Lying, 20

M

magnet, 49
male, 26, 27
manipulate, 12, 26, 41
manipulation, 7, 32, 46
manipulative, 12, 13
mankind, 47
married, 12, 28, 42, 44, 46, 59
mature, 14
Meekness, 8
Men, 3, 25, 27, 46
mental issues, 33
mentality, 1, 5, 12, 25
Mentality, 3, 4, 11, 49
mentee, 50
mentor, 28, 59
Merab, 29

mercy, 23, 53
message, 35, 50
messengers, 27, 28, 30
messiness, 7
Michal, 30
mighty, 13
ministry, 39, 45, 59, 60, 62
miracle, 15, 28
miracles, 60
miserable, 9
mistreat, 9
mocked, 30, 31
money, 26, 41, 44, 45
mother, 13, 57, 59
motive, 10, 39
Mount Sinai, 47
mouth, 16, 20, 24
Mr. Hyde, 42
Mr. Jekyll, 42
murders, 8

N

Naaman, 28
Nabal, 27, 28
narcissist, 6, 37, 38, 39
narcissistic personality, 6
Narcs, 38
nationalities, 56

nations, 57, 59
natural, 18
needy, 14
negative energy, 9
negativity, 26
neighbor, 12
new beginnings, 54
new creature, 54
non-Christians, 1
non-religious, 5
nose, 41

O

Obsession, 49
offended, 16
old man, 54
Oscar, 5
overcome, 15, 33
oxymoron, 10

P

pain, 22
pardon, 53
passion, 56
passive aggressive, 26
patient, 9
peace, 8

peacemakers, 9
pedestals, 42
people, 1, 2, 5, 6, 7, 9, 10, 14, 15, 16, 18, 22, 23, 25, 26, 27, 34, 38, 39, 40, 42, 44, 45, 47, 50, 51, 52, 55, 56, 57, 60
performance, 26
persecute, 35
personality disorders, 6
perversion, 17
Pharisees, 53
Philistine, 13, 30
Philistines, 29
phone, 35
poor, 41
positive direction, 32
pout, 17
powers, 18
praise, 15, 16
pray, 14, 15, 17, 18, 22, 33, 34, 35, 36, 52
prayer, 4, 18, 46, 51, 52, 53
Prayer, 34
prayer life, 4
prayers, 34, 52, 53
preach, 41, 44, 46
preaching, 23, 45, 55, 56
preaching style, 23
pretty girl, 16
prey, 13
price, 45

Pride, 10, 15, 52
prideful, 27
principalities, 18
principle, 51
prison, 13
probation, 17
problem, 9, 11, 20, 40
promises, 44
promote, 16, 34
promotion, 40
prophesy, 44
prophesying, 2, 30, 55
Prophet, 55, 61
Prophetess Kimberly Moses, 1
prophetic destiny, 1
prophets, 30
prostitution, 41
protection, 22
punching bag, 35
pure conscience, 51
purge, 14, 17, 53

Q

qualifications, 39
qualities, 1
Queen Vashti, 12

R

Rachel, 12
radiant, 57
radio, 56
reaction, 18
recognition, 10, 15
rejected, 14, 23
rejection, 22
relationship, 6, 42, 44, 47
religious, 5
repent, 14
Repenting, 53
reputation, 17
resentment, 20
responsibility, 26
revelation, 1, 2
revellings, 8
revenge, 18
rock bottom, 15
Roman Empire, 50
roommate, 47
root, 17, 20
rude, 8, 28, 36
rules, 6

S

sacrifice, 41
Sadducees, 53

safety nets, 36
Samson, 13
Samuel, 21, 29, 30
Satan, 47
satisfaction, 18
satisfied, 11
Saul, 21, 29, 30
scandal, 45
sea of forgetfulness, 53
secret, 13
seditions, 8
seduction, 26
self- preservation, 26
self-centered, 27
Self-centeredness, 7
self-esteem, 7, 16
self-importance, 37
Selfish, 15
selfishness, 15
selfless, 10
self-worth, 16
servant, 15, 47, 52, 60
sex, 46
sexual abuse, 7
signs, 26, 60
silent treatment, 47
sin, 22, 46, 52, 53
singing, 21
sister, 12

situation, 18, 19, 20, 38
social media, 17, 35, 40, 50
soul, 42, 54
South Carolina, 59
space, 32, 35
spear, 29, 30
spirit, 9, 18, 23, 27, 29, 34, 35, 39, 54
spiritual cataracts, 34
spiritual wickedness, 18
spotlight, 16, 40, 43
spouse, 46
stagnant, 5
stranger, 16, 42, 47
strangers, 17
strength, 9, 10, 52
stress, 33
strife, 8
strong, 26, 51, 55, 57
submission, 40
success, 17
suffered, 7, 13
suicide, 30
superficial, 54
supernatural, 23, 55
support, 17
swallow, 17
symptoms, 21, 24, 54

T

tactics, 26
teaches, 1, 50
team, 16
tear, 9, 42
temperance, 8
temple, 45
tempt, 47
tendency, 26
the Christian drama queen mentality, 1
therapy, 33
thousand dollars, 46
threatened, 17, 40
throw stuff, 17
Timothy, 50, 51
title, 8
tongues, 23, 39
toxic, 38
traits, 14
transformation, 50
transgressions, 53
transplant, 20
travel, 44
trouble, 11, 32, 50
trust, 5, 18, 20, 45, 51

U

unadulterated truth, 55

uncleanness, 8
uncomfortable, 17
unimportant, 43
unrealistic demands, 9, 40
unrighteous man, 53
unstable, 6
upper hand, 13

V

validation, 4, 5, 14
variance, 8
vengeful, 12
vessel, 14, 55, 57
Vessel, 55
victim, 14, 32
video, 2
vindication, 18
vineyard, 12, 27
violence, 26

W

weakness, 13
wealth, 41
weapon, 46
web, 13, 20, 32
weighty presence, 2
white lies, 20

wholeness, 54
wicked, 22, 52, 53
wife, 12, 28, 44
wisdom, 33, 35, 36, 55
wise, 26, 36
witchcraft, 8
witness, 36
women, 1, 2, 8, 9, 12, 13, 21, 25, 26, 29, 46, 59
worshipping, 10
wrath, 8
wrestle, 18

Y

yell, 17
yielded, 15

www.ingramcontent.com/pod-product-compliance
Lightning Source LLC
Chambersburg PA
CBHW052116110526
44592CB00013B/1633